D1737411

Religions of the World

Christianity

Rita Faelli

MEDIA ENHANCED BOOKS
AV²
BY WEIGL™
ADDED VALUE • AUDIO VISUAL

Go to www.av2books.com, and enter this book's unique code.

BOOK CODE

U 6 9 3 3 3 9

AV² by Weigl brings you media enhanced books that support active learning.

AV² provides enriched content that supplements and complements this book. Weigl's AV² books strive to create inspired learning and engage young minds in a total learning experience.

Your AV² Media Enhanced books come alive with...

Audio
Listen to sections of the book read aloud.

Key Words
Study vocabulary, and complete a matching word activity.

Video
Watch informative video clips.

Quizzes
Test your knowledge.

Embedded Weblinks
Gain additional information for research.

Slide Show
View images and captions, and prepare a presentation.

Try This!
Complete activities and hands-on experiments.

... and much, much more!

Published by AV² by Weigl
350 5th Avenue, 59th Floor
New York, NY 10118
Website: www.av2books.com

Library of Congress Control Number: 2015942085

ISBN 978-1-4896-4027-7 (hardcover)
ISBN 978-1-4896-4028-4 (soft cover)
ISBN 978-1-4896-4029-1 (single user eBook)
ISBN 978-1-4896-4030-7 (multi-user eBook)

Printed in the United States of America in Brainerd, Minnesota
1 2 3 4 5 6 7 8 9 0 19 18 17 16 15

052015
052215

Photo Credits

The publisher gratefully acknowledges the photo suppliers for this title: Getty Images, pages 1, 5; Dale Robins, page 6; Newspix, page 7; Salvation Army, page 10; Greg Nichols, page 11b; Paula Rusyanto, page 11c; Bobbie Osbourne, Anglican Dioses Melbourne, pages 14, 18, 20, 21, 28, 29; image*after, pg 17b; Terry Healy, page 23; Sal Sen, page 25; Stole Edstrom, page 26. All other photographs and illustrations are © copyright UC Publishing Pty Ltd.

Every reasonable effort has been made to trace ownership and to obtain permission to reprint copyright material. The publishers would be pleased to have any errors or omissions brought to their attention so that they may be corrected in subsequent printings.

Contents

What Is Christianity?

Christianity is the world's largest religion. It began about 2,000 years ago in the Middle East. It is now the major religion in many parts of the world.

Christianity is based on the teachings and life of Jesus **Christ**. People who follow Christianity are called Christians.

Word fact

The word "Christ" is a special title that means king or messiah.
A messiah is someone who is sent by God to save the world.

Many Christians consider Vatican City a holy place. Vatican City is home to Saint Peter's Basilica, which honors an important follower of Jesus.

Jesus Christ

Jesus was born about 2,000 years ago in Bethlehem, a town in the Middle East. He spent his life helping people and teaching them to love God and to respect each other.

Jesus was brought up in the Jewish religion by his parents, Mary and Joseph. When he was about 30 years old, he travelled throughout the region, working miracles and telling people about God and how to live their lives. He chose 12 men to help him. These men were called his **disciples**.

Fast fact
Scenes from Jesus' life are often shown on stained-glass windows in churches.

Jesus' teachings often upset the local religious leaders and the Romans who were in charge of his country at the time. They arrested him and sentenced him to death by **crucifixion**.

Christians believe that, three days after his death, Jesus returned to life. He told his disciples to go and teach others about him. Then he rose into heaven. Christians call this Christ's **Resurrection**.

After this, Jesus' disciples took his teachings to other lands. They set up churches throughout the **Roman Empire**.

Fast fact
There is a church in Bethlehem at the site where Christians believe Jesus was born. It is a special place for **pilgrims** to visit.

Different Christian Groups

Over the centuries, different Christian groups developed their own ideas about practising the Christian religion.

Some Christians are Roman Catholic, under the leadership of the Pope. Some Christians are Orthodox, while others are Protestant. These groups have different histories and traditions but they all share the main Christian beliefs.

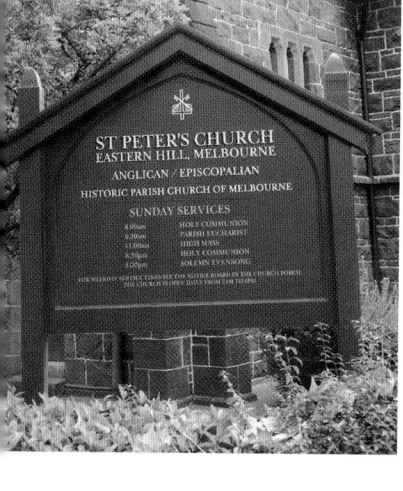

What Do Christians Believe?

Christians believe that God came to Earth in human form as Jesus Christ.

Christians believe that there is one God, who made the universe and everything in it.

However, they believe that God is made up of three aspects: God the Father, who made the universe; God the Son, Jesus Christ; and God the Holy Spirit. This is called the **Trinity**.

Christians also believe that after Jesus died, God brought him back to life. This is called the Resurrection.

Christians try to follow the example of Jesus, who showed the importance of respecting and helping other people. There are many Christian charities all over the world, helping people in need.

Fast fact

The Salvation Army is a religious group that is well known for its charity work.

Jesus told his followers to pray to God. Christians can pray anywhere. They can come together at churches and they can pray in their own home. People can read prayers out of books, recite special prayers or make up their own prayers as they go along.

Fast fact
Some people use **rosary beads** to help them pray.

What Are the Christian Holy Books?

The most important holy book for Christians is the **Bible**. The Bible is a collection of books written over more than one thousand years.

The Bible is divided into two parts – the **Old Testament** and the **New Testament**. The Old Testament was written before Jesus was born and tells the stories of Jewish history and laws. The New Testament tells the story about Jesus' life, teachings and works.

Recently, some other sacred writings from the time of Jesus have been found. These are called the **Dead Sea Scrolls**. Scholars are studying them to see what new history they hold.

Fast facts

- The Bible has been translated into 2,000 languages.
- There is at least one copy in every church.
- It was first printed in English in 1535.
- It is made up of 66 books written by different writers.
- It was written over about 1,000 years.
- It is made up of stories, poems, **psalms**, prayers, laws and letters.

Where Do Christians Worship?

Christians worship at home and in churches. A **church** is a special building in which people pray and worship God.

On the outside, churches can look very different. However, most churches have a cross on the building or close to the building. This shows that it is a place where Christ is worshipped.

Fast fact

An important Christian symbol is the cross. It is a reminder that Jesus Christ died on the cross.

Large churches are called cathedrals.

Baptist churches can be called tabernacles.

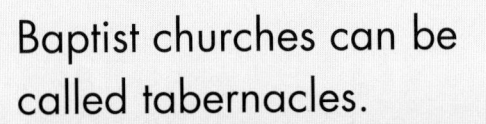

Quakers call their buildings meeting houses.

Small churches are called chapels.

Inside a Church

On the inside, churches can be quite different. However, there are some things that are common to many churches.

▲ An **altar** is a table used for religious ceremonies.

▼ Pews are long, wooden seats.

▲ A **pulpit** is used by the person who is giving a special talk or **sermon**.

▼ A font is a special bowl that holds water that has been blessed.

17

Christian Religious Leaders

Just as there are different groups of Christians, there are also different names for Christian religious leaders.

Depending on the group, religious leaders may be called priests, ministers, vicars or pastors. These people are responsible for teaching the Christian message, and for giving advice and help to church members. Some groups, but not all, only allow men to be leaders.

Religious leaders have many responsibilities, including:

- leading services
- leading church meetings during the week
- visiting sick people at home
- baptizing people
- marrying people
- conducting funerals.

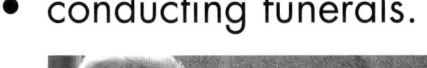

Fast fact
In some churches there are people, other than the leaders, who dedicate their entire lives to God. Some of these people are called nuns or monks.

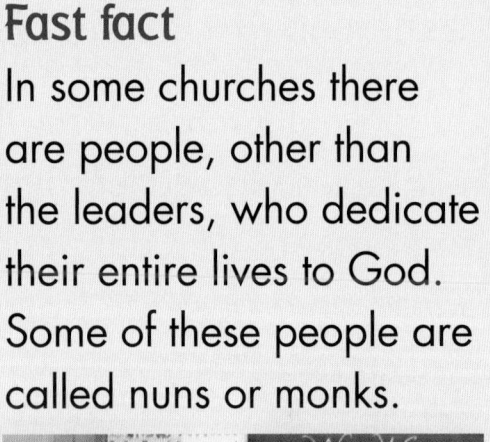

The Church Service

The most important day of worship for Christians is Sunday. Christians believe Sunday is special because it is the day when Jesus rose from the dead.

During a church service, there is usually singing of religious songs called hymns, readings from the Bible and prayers. The religious leader usually gives a talk based on a passage from the Bible, to the congregation.

Holy Communion

For many Christian groups, but not all, one of the most important parts of a church service is **Holy Communion**.

During communion, wine and special bread is blessed by the religious leader, who then shares the bread and wine with the people at the church. Eating the bread and drinking the wine is symbolic of the last time Jesus ate with his disciples – the Last Supper.

> **Word facts**
>
> Names for communion include Mass, Eucharist, Holy Communion and the Lord's Supper.

Saints

In the Christian religion, a saint is someone who has given his or her life to serve God.

These people are believed to be very holy and when they die they are given a special place in heaven. Because saints are so close to God, Christians pray to them.

Fast facts

One well-known saint is Saint Francis of Assisi. He showed special kindness to animals. Every year on Saint Francis Day, people often ask priests to bless their pets.

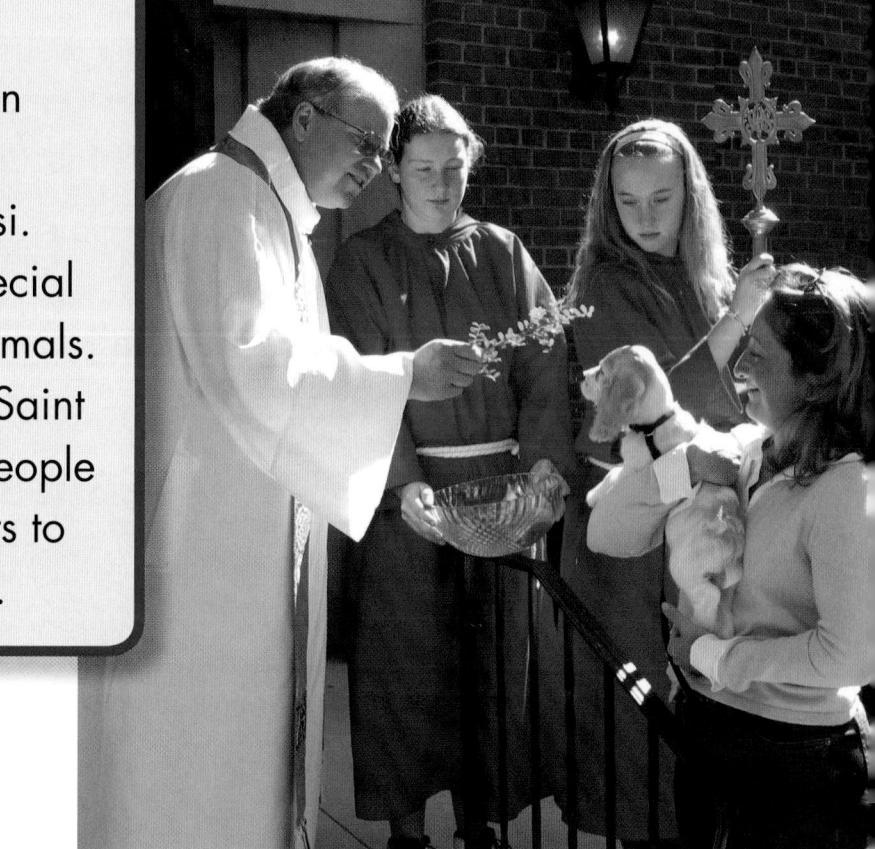

Baptism

Christians celebrate different events in their lives with a religious ceremony. For many Christians, **baptism** (also called christening in some Christian churches) is a special service that celebrates someone joining a Christian church.

Baptism, or christening, usually occurs when the person is a baby. The parents choose two people to be the baby's godparents. The godparents promise to bring the child up to follow the church's teachings. The religious leader says special words and blesses the baby with holy water.

Fast facts

- A few churches, for example the Baptists, only baptize adults.
- The Salvation Army and the Quakers do not baptize people.

Confirmation

Another important event for many Christians is **confirmation**.

Confirmation is usually made when boys and girls are between 10 and 13 years old. At confirmation, boys and girls reaffirm the promises made on their behalf when they were baptized.

Marriage

Many Christians get married in church. They want their marriage to be a religious celebration, as well as a legal one.

For a wedding, the church is usually decorated with lots of flowers so that it looks beautiful. The couple stand at the front of the church and the religious leader performs the marriage ceremony.

Death

Christians believe that death is the beginning of a new life with God.

When somebody dies, a special service called a funeral is held. The coffin is placed in the church and the religious leader conducts the service with prayers, hymns and a sermon or a talk based on the Bible.

Christmas

Christmas celebrates the birth of Jesus on December 25th.

A special church service is held. There are readings from the Bible about Jesus' life and special Christmas hymns called carols are sung. It is a very joyful time.

Fast fact

At Christmas, many Christian children take part in plays that tell the story of the birth of Jesus. These are called nativity plays.

Word fact

The word Christmas comes from "Christ's mass".

Lent and Holy Week

Lent is a time for Christians to think about the things they have done wrong and to be truly sorry.

Lent starts six weeks before **Easter**. The last week of Lent is called Holy Week. Many important events take place during this time.

During Holy Week, on Good Friday, many churches hold processions called the Stations of the Cross. Christians remember the death of Jesus with the processions.

Easter

Easter Day is the most important holy day for Christians. On this day, they celebrate the Resurrection of Jesus.

Different churches have their own way of celebrating. Some go to church on Easter Sunday to celebrate the Resurrection of Christ. After church, people go home and have a Sunday feast. Some people give special eggs to their friends and families.

Key Words

altar a table used in religious ceremonies in a church

baptism a religious ceremony to welcome someone joining the Christian faith

Bible the Christian holy book, made up of the Old Testament and the New Testament

Christ a special title that means king or messiah

church Christian place of worship

confirmation religious ceremony for boys and girls when they formally join the Christian faith

crucifixion a method of killing someone used in ancient times

Dead Sea Scrolls ancient writings on scrolls

disciple one of the first 12 men chosen by Jesus to help him

Easter religious day that celebrates the Resurrection of Jesus

Holy Communion important part of a church service

Lent the 40 days before Easter

New Testament the part of the Bible that tells the stories of Jesus' life

Old Testament the part of the Bible that was written before Jesus was born and tells the stories of Jewish history

pilgrims religious people who travel a long way to a holy place

psalms songs or poems praising God

pulpit a raised structure in a church that is used by the person who is giving the sermon or a special talk

Resurrection Jesus' return to life after his death

Roman Empire lands ruled by ancient Rome

rosary beads string of beads used by some Christians to pray

sermon a talk given as part of a Christian church service

Trinity three parts of the Christian God: the Father, the Son (Jesus), and the Holy Spirit

Index

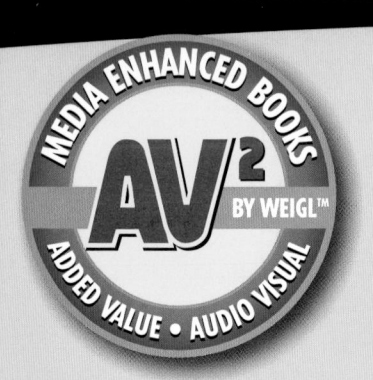

Log on to www.av2books.com

AV² by Weigl brings you media enhanced books that support active learning. Go to www.av2books.com, and enter the special code found on page 2 of this book. You will gain access to enriched and enhanced content that supplements and complements this book. Content includes video, audio, weblinks, quizzes, a slide show, and activities.

AV² Online Navigation

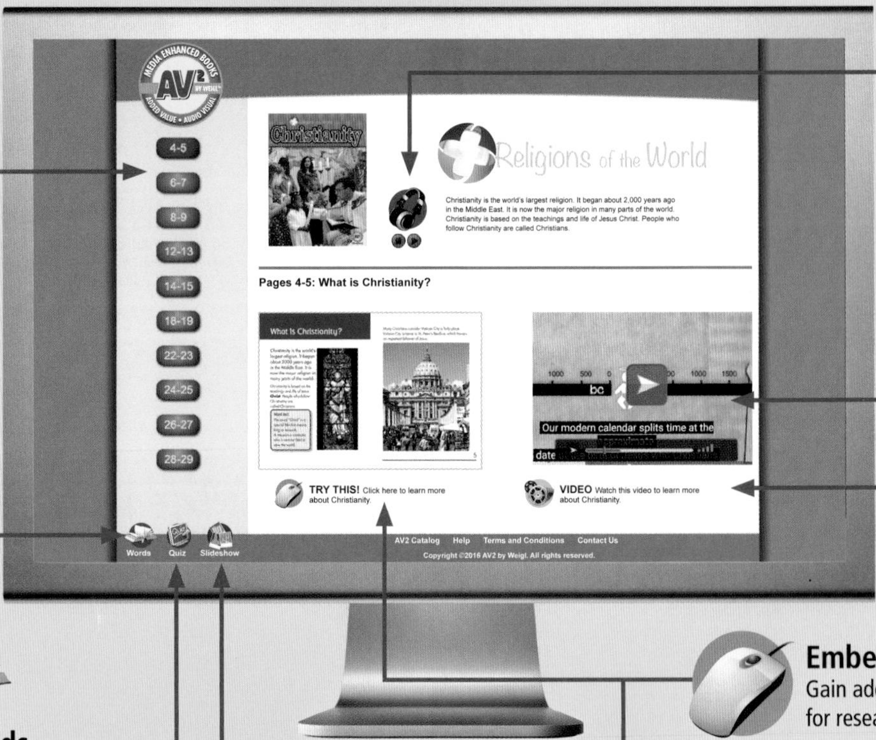

Book Pages
AV² pages directly correspond to pages in the book.

Audio
Listen to sections of the book read aloud.

Video
Watch informative video clips.

Embedded Weblinks
Gain additional information for research.

Key Words
Study vocabulary, and complete a matching word activity.

Try This!
Complete activities and hands-on experiments.

Quizzes
Test your knowledge.

Slide Show
View images and captions, and prepare a presentation.

AV² was built to bridge the gap between print and digital. We encourage you to tell us what you like and what you want to see in the future.

Sign up to be an AV² Ambassador at www.av2books.com/ambassador.